DAILY

VAGUS NERVE

EXERCISES GUIDE

DISCLAIMER NOTICE

This book is not intended as a substitute for the medical advice of physicians. The reader should consult a physician in matters relating to his/her health and particularly with respect to any symptoms that may require diagnosis or medical attention.

This book is not intended as a substitute for the medical advice of physicians. The reader should consult a physician in matters relating to his/her health and particularly with respect to any symptoms that may require diagnosis or medical attention. All the informations contained in this book is for educational and entertainment purposes only. All effort has been done to present accurate, up to date, reliable and complete informations. No warranties of any kind are declared or implied. Readers acknowledge that the author is not engaged in the rendering of derived of any medical or professional advice. The content within this book has been derived from various sources. Please consult a licensed professional before attempting any techniques illustrated in this book

By reading this document, the reader agrees that under no circumstances is the author responsible for any losses, direct or indirect, that are incurred as a result of the use of the information contained within this document, including, but not limited to, errors, omissions or inaccuracies.

Before to begin..

For you a free copy of

"**10 Minutes Stretching for Beginners**" as a **Bonus!**

My guide to start practice stretching from scratch

(Priced 12.99$ on Amazon)

You will find the QR code at the end of the book!

scan the QR code and subscribe to the Newsletter to not miss out on useful tips and lots of news coming out!

Contents

INTRODUCTION

Have you ever heard of the vagus nerve? Well, Either you did or not, this is the opportunity to get to know it and the multiple action it is involved in. The vagus nerve is a long and complex nerve that travels from the brainstem through the neck and into the chest and abdomen, playing a crucial role in regulating a wide range of bodily functions, including digestion, heart rate, and immune response. Recent research has also linked the vagus nerve to mental health and emotional regulation, suggesting that its activation through exercises and practices can improve overall well-being and reduce stress.

In this book, we will explore the benefits of vagus nerve exercises and provide a comprehensive guide to various techniques that can stimulate and strengthen this vital nerve. Drawing on the latest scientific research and the wisdom of ancient healing practices, we will offer step-by-step instructions and practical tips for integrating vagus nerve exercises into your daily routine, from breathing techniques and meditation to physical exercises and dietary changes.

Whether you are seeking to alleviate stress, improve digestion, or enhance emotional resilience, this book will provide you with the tools and knowledge you need to harness the power of the vagus nerve and unlock its full potential for health and well-being.

USE THIS BOOK

Exercise it includes also heart, lungs, and digestive system.
This exercises book can help you improve the health of your vagus nerve and enhance your overall well-being.
Here are some steps to effectively use a book of vagus nerve exercises:

1: Start by reading the introduction and background information: The first step in using a book of vagus nerve exercises is to read the introduction and background information. This will give you a better understanding of what the vagus nerve is, what it does, and why it's essential to your health.

2: Understand the exercises: Next, read through the different exercises provided in the book. Take the time to understand each exercise and how it is meant to benefit the vagus nerve, don't rush is the key.
Make sure you are comfortable with each exercise and can perform it correctly.

3: Create a routine: Once you have read through the exercises, it's time to create a routine.
You will find a pre-made routine at the end of the book, some a samples that you can use to make it on your own.
Choose the exercises that work best for you and your schedule, and make sure to include the ones that can suit you at the best.

4: Start slow: It's important to start slow and not push yourself too hard when starting a new routine. Begin with a few exercises and gradually increase the number and intensity over time.

5: Track your progress: Keep a record of your progress. This will help you to track your improvements and to see which exercises are working best for you.
You will also find some tables in which you can note your progress at the end of the book

6: Incorporate other lifestyle changes: To enhance the benefits of the vagus nerve exercises, consider incorporating other lifestyle changes, such as reducing stress, improving sleep, and eating a healthy diet.
You will find a specific section and some useful tips within the book

IMPORTANT!

Seek professional help: If you have any underlying health conditions or concerns, it's important to seek professional help before starting any new exercise routine. A doctor or other health professional can provide guidance on the best exercises and precautions to take in case of injuries and chronic illness.

Remember that..
The benefits of vagus nerve exercises may not be immediate, but with consistency and commitment, you can improve the health of your vagus nerve and enhance your overall wellbeing.

A special dedication to all my pupils

What's the Vagus nerve?

ANATOMY

Also known as the **Pneumogastric nerve**, the **Vagus nerve** (VNS) is one of the twelve pair of **cranial nerves**, the tenth to be exact. The cranial nerves, are fundamental **nerve structures** that arise at the level of the brain and can have a sensory or motor function or both (therefore mixed).
But the vagus nerve, compared to the latters, has a peculiarity, in fact its nucleus of origin is close to other cranial nerves but, unlike the others, the vagus nerve branches downwards.
Along its path it gives rise to various nerve branches, which innervate various organs and tissues including: skin of the external auditory canal, mucosa and muscles of the pharynx and larynx, trachea, bronchi, lungs, heart, large blood vessels, esophagus, stomach and intestine..
The vagus is **the longest** nerve found inside our body, in fact it originates in the medulla oblongata and extends to innervate the main organs, having a role in both the cardiac and **pulmonary** and **digestive systems**.
Among the different mechanisms underlying the communication between the brain and the intestine, the most direct one is certainly the one mediated by the vagus nerve.
The vagus nerve is a mixture of efferent fibers (20%) and afferent fibers (80%). While the former are used to transmit stimuli from the central nervous system to the periphery, the latter transmit information in the opposite direction * [1].

[1. Efferent (or motor) fibers are the nerve pathways that carry the neural message from the central nervous system to the periphery, which they transform into a mechanical response. On the contrary, there are afferent or sensitive ones.]

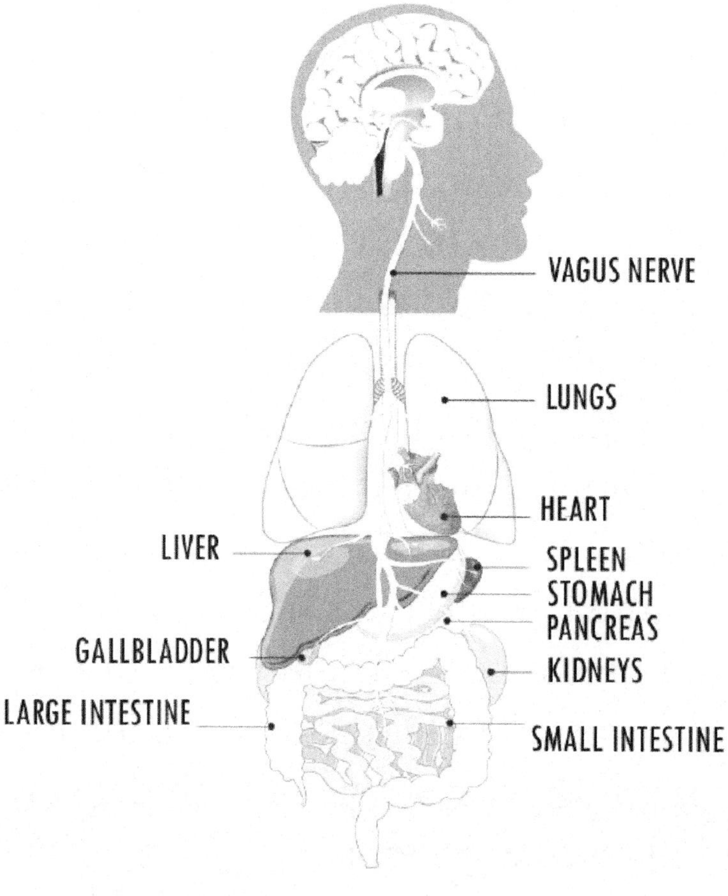

Curiosity

Origin of the name: The term "vago" comes from the Latin word "vagus", which means "vagabond", "wandering". Probably, doctors coined this name in reference to the long and intricate path that the vagus nerve takes within the human body.
The reason behind the use of the term "pneumogastric" is decidedly different. This adjective refers to two important innervations of the vagus nerve: the innervation of the lungs ("pneumo") and the innervation of the stomach ("gastric").

RIGHT AND LEFT VAGUS NERVE

Starting from the base of the neck (therefore also at the thoracic and abdominal level), the right vagus nerve and the left vagus nerve follow a different course, which distinguishes them from each other.
Briefly, the main differences are:

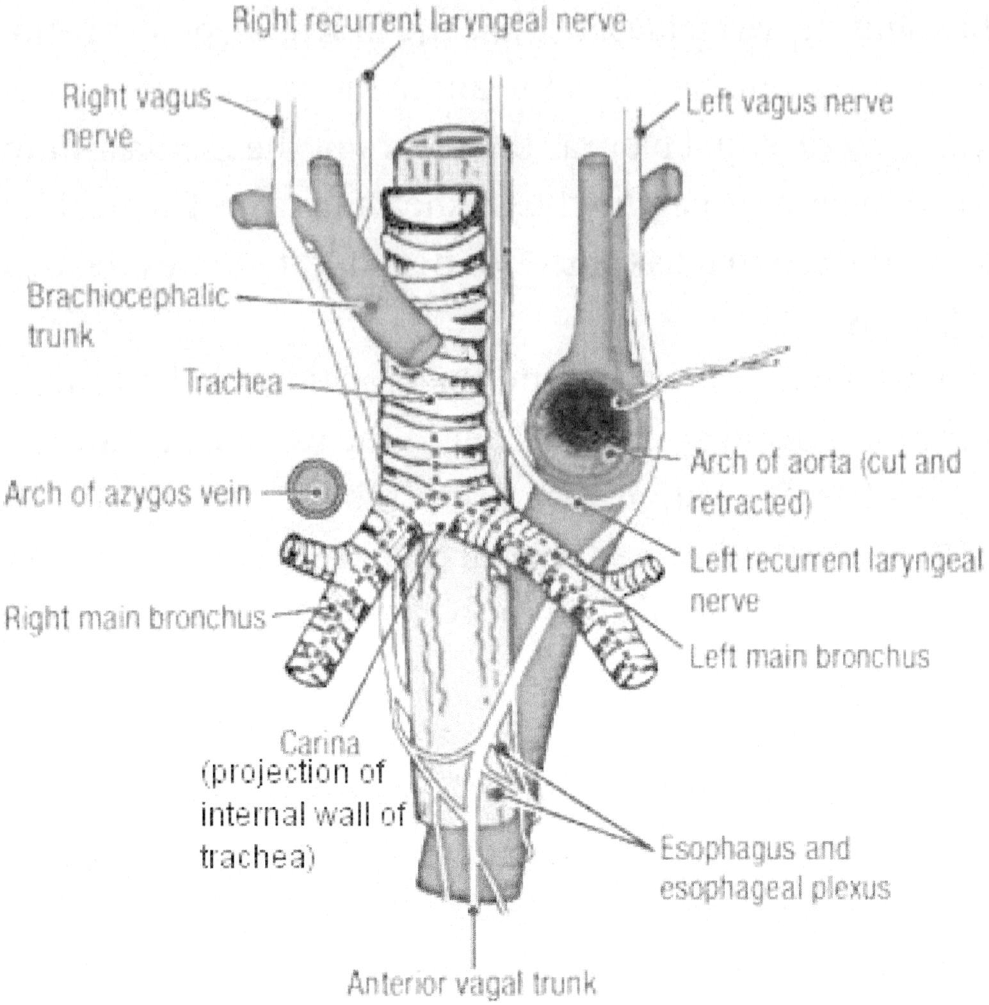

Between neck and chest

- The right vagus nerve resides: behind the anastomosis between the internal jugular vein and the subclavian vein; in a medial position with respect to the pleural dome (ie the tract of parietal pleura that covers the apexes of the lungs); in a lateral position with respect to the common carotid artery; in front of the subclavian artery.
- The left vagus nerve resides: behind the brachiocephalic venous trunk; in a medial position with respect to the pleural dome, the subclavian artery and the phrenic nerve; in a lateral position to the common carotid artery.

Chest area

- The right vagus nerve resides: behind the brachiocephalic venous trunk, the superior vena cava and the anonymous artery; in a medial position to the mediastinal pleura (the pleura of the mediastinum); in a lateral position with respect to the trachea and laterotracheal lymph nodes; behind the esophagus (glued to the latter it crosses the orifice, or hiatus, esophagus).
- The left vagus nerve resides: behind the brachiocephalic venous trunk and the common carotid artery; in front of the left subclavian artery and esophagus; in a lateral position with respect to the trachea; in a medial position with respect to the mediastinal pleura and the phrenic nerve; in front of the esophagus (attached to the latter it crosses the orifice, or hiatus, esophagus).

Abdomen area

- The right vagus nerve passes behind the cardia the valve that separates the esophagus from the stomach and ends at the celiac plexus, which resides near the celiac artery.
- The left vagus nerve runs anteriorly through the abdominal portion of the esophagus, then crosses the border of the cardia and finally ends with the branches of the anterior gastric plexus and the hepatic branches.

Vagus nerve's branches

• At the level of the jugular foramen, there is only one branch: the so-called auricular branch. This innervates the skin of the external auditory canal.

• At the level of the neck, the branches are: the pharyngeal branches (which contribute to the formation of the pharyngeal and intercarotid plexuses), the superior laryngeal nerve (which forms the superior laryngeal branch and the inferior laryngeal branch), the recurrent laryngeal nerve (also called inferior) and the superior cardiac nerve (which gives rise to 2-3 branches).

• At the level of the thorax, the branches are: the lower cardiac branch (the right and the left one converge in the so-called cardiac plexus), the anterior bronchial branches (which contribute to the formation of the anterior pulmonary plexus), the posterior bronchial branches (which contribute to the posterior pulmonary plexus) and the anterior and posterior esophageal branches (ending in the esophageal plexus).

• At the level of the abdomen, the branching system is somewhat complicated; in fact it includes:

• The gastric branches of the right vagus nerve, which give rise to the posterior gastric plexus, and the gastric branches of the left vagus nerve, which form the anterior gastric plexus.
• The celiac branches, which originate mainly from the right vagus nerve and form the so-called celiac plexus (or solar plexus).
• The hepatic branches, which arise mainly from the left vagus nerve and give rise to the so-called hepatic plexus.

PARASYMPATHETIC SYSTEM AND FUNCTIONALITY

The vagus nerve (VNS) is part of the **parasympathetic** nervous system which, together with the **sympathetic** nervous system, forms the autonomic nervous system [3].
The parasympathetic nervous system is mainly constituted by the fibers of the vagus nerve (They make it up for 75%) and constitutes, together with the sympathetic nervous system, the so-called **autonomic** or **vegetative** nervous system (ANS), which carries out a control action on all those no-voluntary control functions as as breathing, heartbeat and metabolic processes. Originating in the central nervous system (some of its nerves originate from the brain stem, others from the spinal cord), the **parasympathetic** nervous system fulfills various functions: it stimulates stillness, relaxation, rest, digestion and energy absorption.

The parasympathetic nervous system functions is involves:
the narrowing of the pupil (miosis), the increase in **digestive secretions** (from salivary, gastric and biliary to enteric and pancreatic ones), the increase in **peristaltic activity** (promoting the motility of the wall intestinal), decrease in heart rate, contraction of bronchial muscles, relaxation of the bladder sphincter (thus facilitating urination), dilation of blood vessels present on skeletal muscles and stimulation of erection.

All this means that the nerve fibers of the parasympathetic nervous system are distributed to the eyes, salivary glands, numerous abdominal organs (stomach, intestines, liver, etc.), the heart, lungs, blood vessels and genital organs.
From a comparison between the parasympathetic and sympathetic systems, it can be immediately noted that the latter performs an activity diametrically opposite to the former, as it has stimulating, exciting and contracting functions (after all it presides over the adaptation system known as "attack and leak").

Functions of sympathetic and Parasympathetic nervous system

	SYMPATHETIC	PARASYMPATHETIC
EYE	dilatation (mydriasis)	constriction (miosis)
SALIVARY GLANDS	mucus secretion	watery secretion
HEART	increases frequency and force of contraction	reduces frequency
ARTERIES AND VEINS	vasoconstricts	reduces frequency
LUNGS	bronchodilation	bronchoconstriction
DIGESTIVE TRACT	decreases motility and secretion	increases motility and secretion
PANCREAS	inhibits insulin secretion	stimulates insulin secretion
BLADDER	inhibits urination	stimulates urination

Reading the anatomy of the vagus nerve, its complexity that derives from its many and varied functions clearly emerges, let's try to list some of them in a simple way..

The functions of the vagus nerve can be divided into:

▹ Parasympathetic precisely, for the smooth muscles of the thoracic and abdominal viscera, with particular importance for the heart, it's the most important function. The parasympathetic nervous system forms the autonomic nervous system, together with the sympathetic nervous system, with which they regulate the involuntary functions of the organism. Among the main functions of the parasympathetic system we find

- Heart rate threshold (bradycardia),
- Increased secretions of the digestive tract (salivary, gastric, pancreatic, biliary and intestinal),
- Increased intestinal peristalsis, promoting digestion,
- Contraction of the bronchial muscles,
- Dilation of innervated arterial vessels (vasodilation);

- ***Palate lift,***
- ***Salpingopharyngeal,***
- ***Palatopharyngeal,***
- ***Pharyngeal constrictors,***
- ***Intrinsic pharyngeal muscles,***
- ***Palatoglossus.***

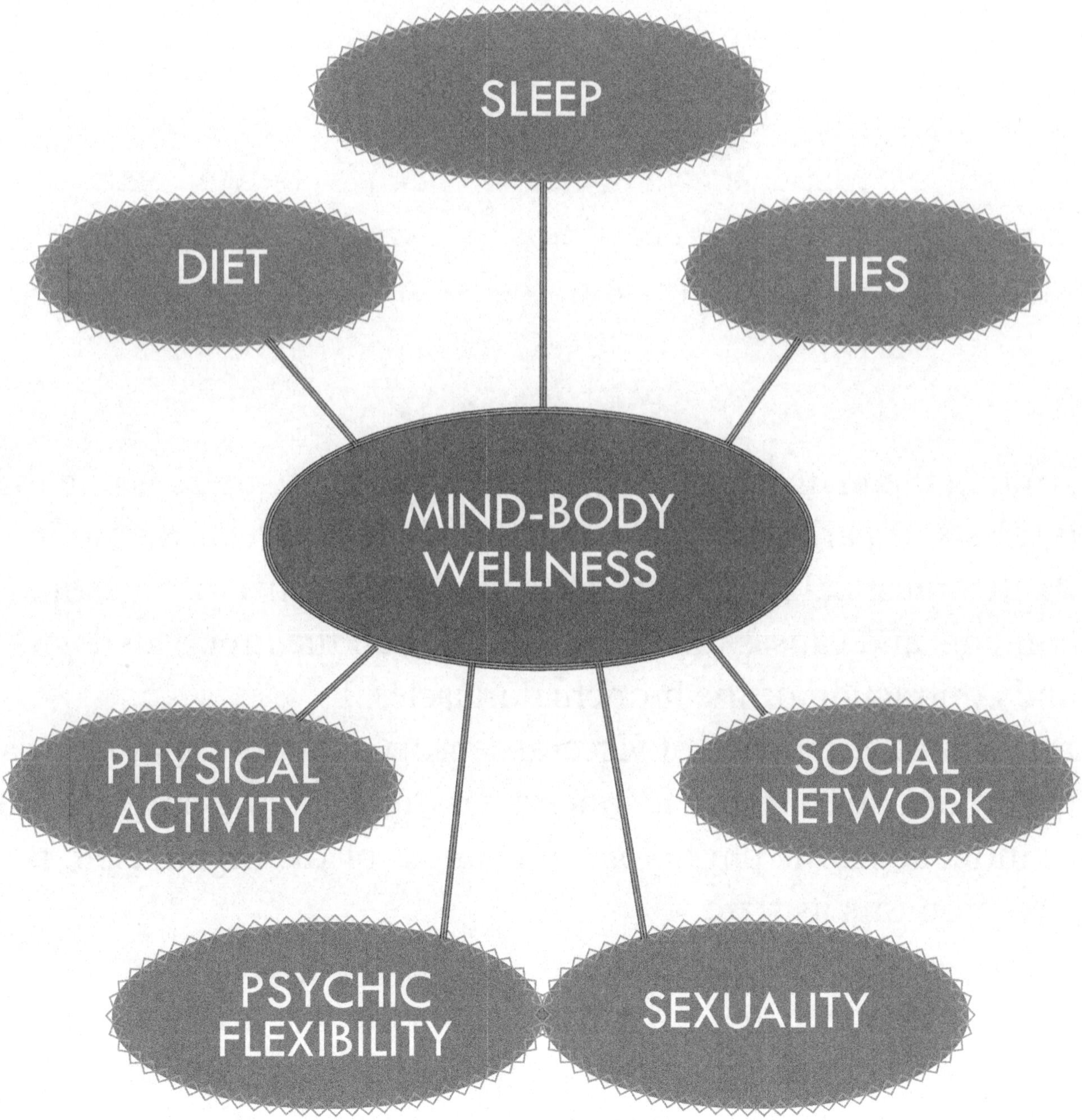
SLEEP
DIET
TIES
MIND-BODY WELLNESS
PHYSICAL ACTIVITY
SOCIAL NETWORK
PSYCHIC FLEXIBILITY
SEXUALITY

THE GUT-BRAIN CONNECTION

The vagus nerve plays a critical role in the gut-brain axis, which is the bidirectional communication pathway between our gut and our brain. In this chapter, we'll look at the ways in which the vagus nerve interacts with the gut microbiome and how this can impact our overall health and wellbeing.

Among the many functions of the vagus nerve, there is one that interests us particularly: the one that directly affects digestion. At the intestinal level, peristalsis increases, transit of intestinal contents and causes the vasodilation of all the innervated vessels and contraction of the bronchial muscles.
It has another important visceral sensory function, that is, it carries information from the innervated organs to the brain, as well as influencing the physiological changes of the organ itself, it also monitors its state.

Furthermore, when the brain perceives that we are in a situation of relaxation it communicates it to the Parasympathetic Nervous System and therefore also to the Vagus Nerve which is part of it and which implements its functions to promote digestion. How? Increasing gastric acid and intestinal peristalsis. It receives sensitive information from the meninges and mucous membranes of the digestive tract, exploiting its general somatic sensory function.

On the other hand, in fact, when you are in a moment of stress and anxiety, the brain goes haywire and sends confused messages to the Vagus Nerve which no longer performs its functions optimally, digestion is particularly affected and the following can be felt symptoms:

- ***Stomach acid***
- ***Nausea***
- ***Abdominal swelling***
- ***Intestinal swelling***

The opposite is also true, however: a constant state of irritation in the stomach and intestines can have negative effects on the activity of the vagus nerve.
This is why nutrition is an important tool for normalizing vagal functions at the digestive level

It's also responsible for the gustatory perceptions of the tongue (special sensory function).
Being a mixed nerve it also has a motor part dedicated to a series of muscles involved in chewing and swallowing, as well as phonation.

VAGUS NERVE AND CIRCULATION

The vagus nerve (VNS) mediates the entire parasympathetic activity of the **heart**.
Through the right lower heart branch, it innervates the sinoatrial node (SA node), which is the most important of the heart's pacing centers (dominant pacing center).
By means of the left lower cardiac branch, on the other hand, it innervates the atrioventricular node, a pathway center of the secondary heart (therefore less important than the previous one).
Balanced stimulation of the lower cardiac branches is essential so that the heart rate does not undergo an excessive reduction.
In fact, as a result of their hyperstimulation - in particular of the left lower cardiac branch - it's possible that an atrioventricular block condition is established.

Curiosity

The study of cardiac activity in relation to the stimulation of the vagus nerve led to the discovery, by a German pharmacologist named Otto Loewi, of a now well-known chemical neurotransmitter: acetylcholine.
With his experiments (which also allowed him to obtain the Nobel Prize), Loewi proved that:

- The vagus nerve induces bradycardia by releasing acetylcholine.
- Some inhibitors of acetylcholine receptors (muscarinic receptors) interrupt various functions of the vagus nerve, including the bradycardic function.

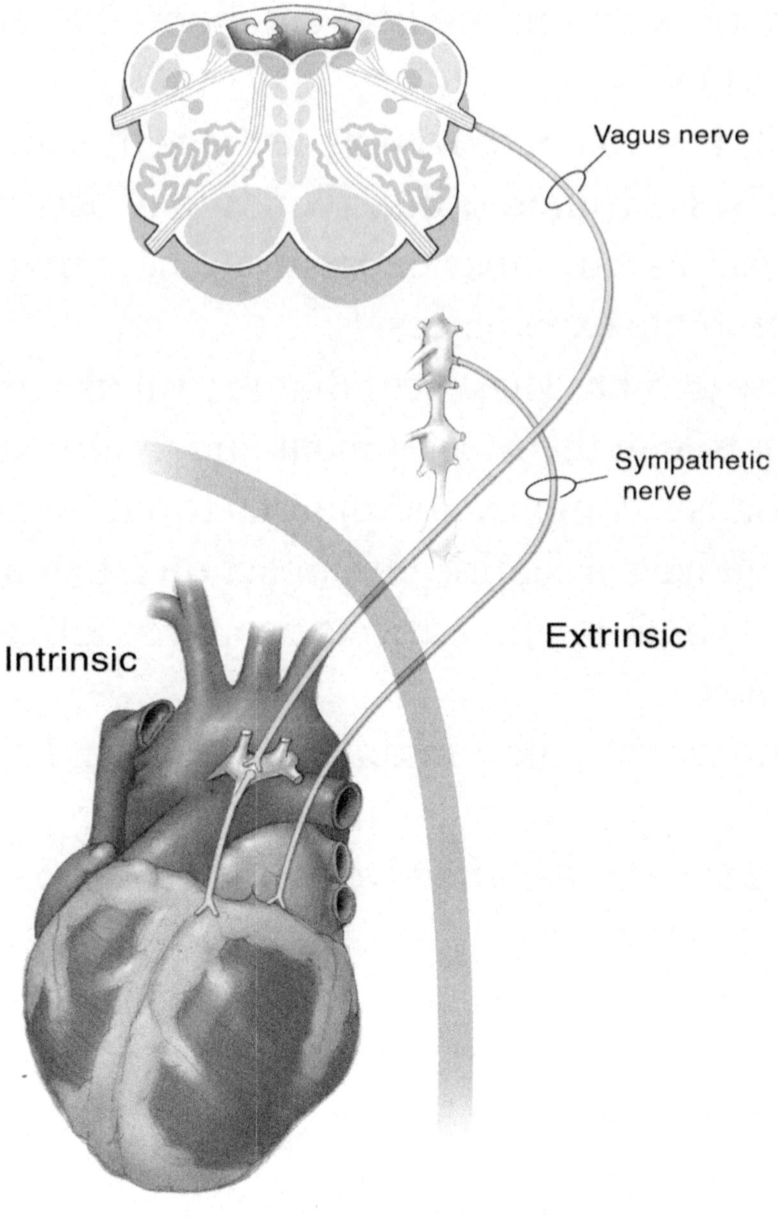
Vagus nerve
Sympathetic
nerve
Extrinsic
Intrinsic

VAGUS NERVE AND DEPRESSION

Depression is a serious medical condition that affects millions of people worldwide.
As known, It is characterized by feelings of sadness, hopelessness, and loss of interest in activities they used to enjoy. Many different factors can cause depression, including genetics, environment and life experiences.
Recent research has suggested that the vagus nerve may play a significant role in the development and treatment of depression.
Depression is a complex and multifactorial mental health disorder that can have a significant impact on a person's daily life. It is a common condition that affects people of all ages, genders, and backgrounds.
Depression can manifest in different ways and can be classified into different types, such as major depressive disorder, bipolar disorder, and seasonal affective disorder.

Symptoms of depression can include persistent feelings of sadness, hopelessness, and helplessness, loss of interest in activities, changes in appetite, and disrupted sleep patterns.
Depression can also affect a person's energy levels, concentration, and ability to function.

VAGUS NERVE AND DEPRESSION CONNECTION

The vagus nerve plays a crucial role in regulating mood and emotions.

It is connected to the limbic system, which is the part of the brain responsible for processing emotions.

Studies have shown that stimulating the vagus nerve can lead to improvements in depression symptoms. In addition, vagus nerve stimulation (VNS) therapy has been used as a treatment option for depression.

VAGUS NERVE STIMULATION (VNS) THERAPY:

VNS therapy is a treatment option for people with treatment-resistant depression. It involves implanting a small device under the skin in the chest area that is connected to the vagus nerve. The device sends electrical impulses to the nerve, which can help regulate mood and reduce symptoms of depression.

The Role of Vagus Nerve in Neurotransmitter Regulation:

The vagus nerve plays a critical role in regulating neurotransmitters, which are chemicals that transmit signals between nerve cells in the brain. Research has shown that the vagus nerve can affect the levels of neurotransmitters such as serotonin, dopamine, and norepinephrine, which are all associated with mood regulation.

Research and Studies:

Several studies have investigated the use of VNS therapy in the treatment of depression. A study published in the Journal of Affective Disorders found that VNS therapy was effective in reducing depression symptoms in patients with treatment-resistant depression.

Another study published in the Journal of Psychiatric Research found that VNS therapy was associated with improved quality of life and reduced suicidal ideation in patients with major depressive disorder.

Other Benefits of Stimulating the Vagus Nerve:

In addition to its role in regulating mood and emotions, stimulating the vagus nerve can have other benefits. Some of these benefits include stress reduction, improved digestion, and reduced inflammation.

Ways to Stimulate the Vagus Nerve:

There are several ways to stimulate the vagus nerve naturally. Some of these methods include breathing exercises, meditation, physical exercise, and massage therapy. These techniques can help regulate the body's autonomic nervous system and reduce stress levels, which can have a positive impact on mental health.

33 Exercises

to get to know your Vagus

HOW TO APPROACH EXERCISES

Remember, it's important to approach these exercises with a positive attitude and listen to your body. Start with simple exercises, practice regularly, and gradually increase the intensity and duration of your practice. If you experience any discomfort or pain during your exercises, take a break and consult with a healthcare professional. Incorporating vagus nerve exercises into your daily routine can help support the health of the vagus nerve and promote overall well-being.

- **Start slowly:** Begin with simple exercises such as deep breathing, which can help stimulate the vagus nerve and promote relaxation. Once you feel comfortable with these exercises, you can gradually increase the intensity and duration of your exercises.
- **Practice regularly**: Consistency is key when it comes to stimulating the vagus nerve. Make a habit of incorporating vagus nerve exercises into your daily routine. Aim to practice for at least 10-15 minutes a day, ideally at the same time each day.
- **Combine different techniques**: There are various exercises and techniques that can help stimulate the vagus nerve, including deep breathing, yoga, meditation, and singing. Combining different techniques can help increase the effectiveness of your practice.
- **Pay attention to your body**: It is important to listen to your body and avoid pushing yourself too hard. If you experience any discomfort or pain during your exercises, take a break and consult with a healthcare professional.
- **Stay positive**: Approach your vagus nerve exercises with a positive attitude and focus on the benefits they can provide for your overall well-being. Consistent practice can help promote relaxation, reduce stress and anxiety, and improve overall health.

SENSORIAL EXERCISES

These exercises consist of stimulating the nerve near its origin, in this case at the base of the ear and neck. Very useful for relaxing after a stressful day

Ear massage 1

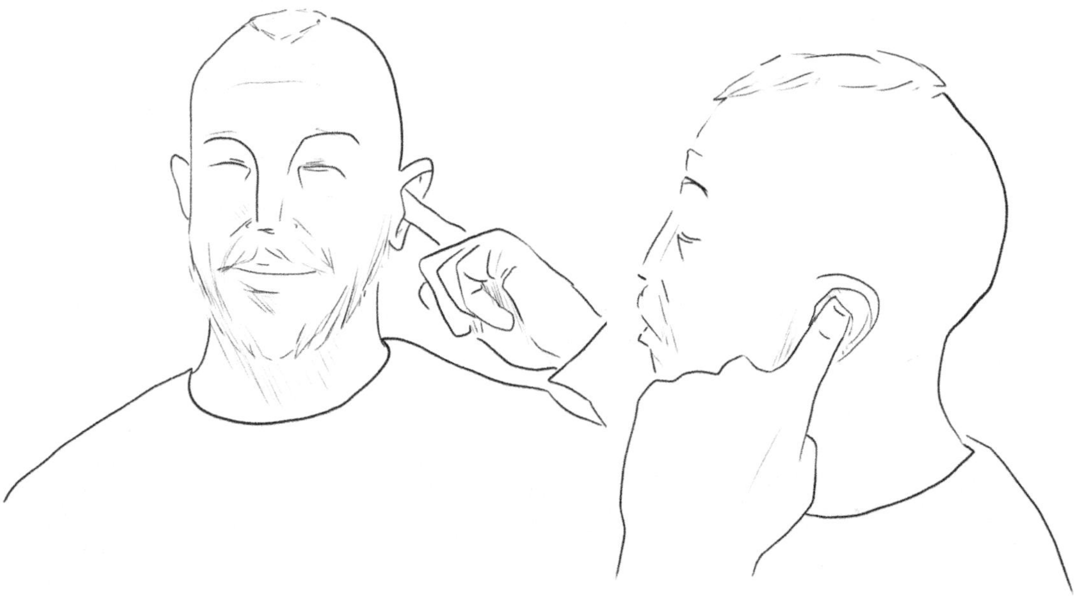

- Insert the index finger of the letf hand into the dimple directly under the antihelix of the ear of the left ear (the outer part of the ear is called the helix, while the inner protuberance is called the antihelix)
- Make circles clockwise and then counterclockwise for about 30 seconds each way, then repeat with the opposite ear

The ear is one of the areas directly related to relaxation, right from infancy, in fact, we can see how infants tend to touch their ears while sleeping or breastfeeding, up to adulthood, when in intimacy with one's partner we feel a pleasant sensation when the ear area is stimulated

Ear massage 2

- Insert the finger of the left hand inside the left ear, but do not push inwards, bend the finger slightly and push backwards
- Apply the right pressure and make circles by massaging the basin (the back of the ear) for about 20 seconds, then reverse the direction of rotation
- Once done, perform with the opposite ear and repeat a total of 2 times per ear

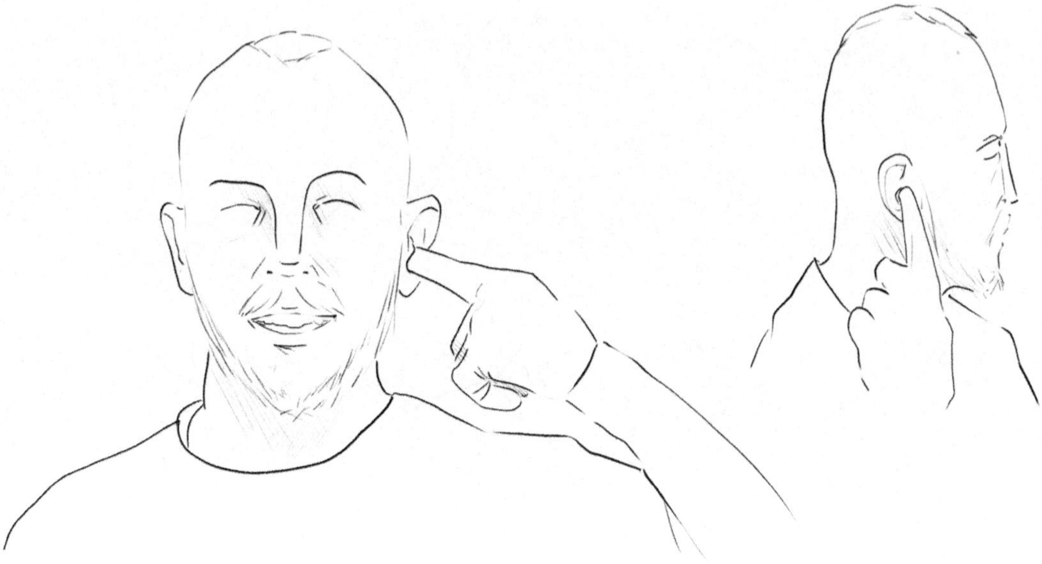

Ear stretch

- Grasp the end of the right ear with the dorsal part of the thumb and the inner part of the index finger and, gently stretch it outward and maintain a constant tension for a few seconds, after which relax it
- Repeat the stretching this time, however, stretching the ear downward, hold the tension a few seconds and repeat by doing the upward stretching
- Perform 2 times for each direction, up, middle and down, after which perform with the other ear

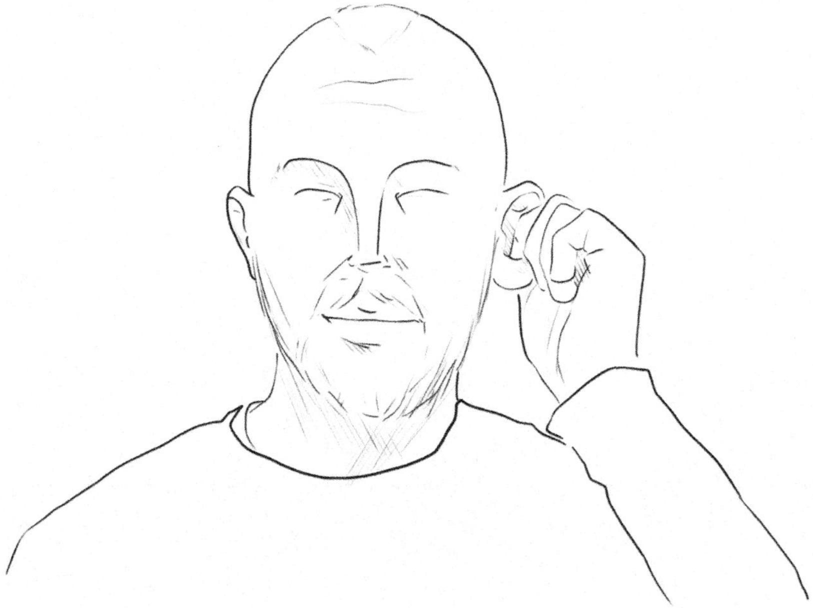

Good exercise also to fight bruxism

Palm pressure

- Place your left hand in the back of the neck behind the left ear and stretch the skin by pulling it backwards with the palm of your hand
- Hold the tension for a few seconds and then relax (you can also make circles with your hand resting on your neck, first in one direction and then in the other)
- Do 4 \ 5 stretches, then perform on the opposite side

- Now place the palm of the left hand on the left side of the nape above the ear, and do the same for 4 \ 5 times (also here you can perform the exercise making circles) and repeat in the opposite side

This is an exercise to stretch all the lateral muscles of the ear

Half tortoise pose

- Sit on a chair maintaining a space of about 8 inches from the backrest, keeping your back and neck straight, feet resting on the floor and hands clinging to the chair.
- Move your feet forward resting them on your heels while extending your legs, after which move them backward moving them under the chair while resting your feet on your toes
- Repeat 12 times for 3 sets

This exercise is also useful for stretch and mobilizing the muscles of the lower back

Excellent exercise for relaxation and extension of the nerve

NECK STIMULATION

One way to stimulate the vagus nerve is certainly through some exercises for the neck, which are very effective even in the case of chronic headaches and frequent stiff necks

Neck turn

- Sit on the floor on your heels resting your knees on the floor.
  Move the left arm behind the back and rest the right hand on the left shoulder so that the shoulder is locked.
  Tilt the neck toward the right shoulder, turn the head to the right

  after which look upward raising the chin we will feel tension in the anterior part of the sternocleidomastoid

- hold the position 30 seconds after which switch sides, and perform 4 times per side

Cervice massage

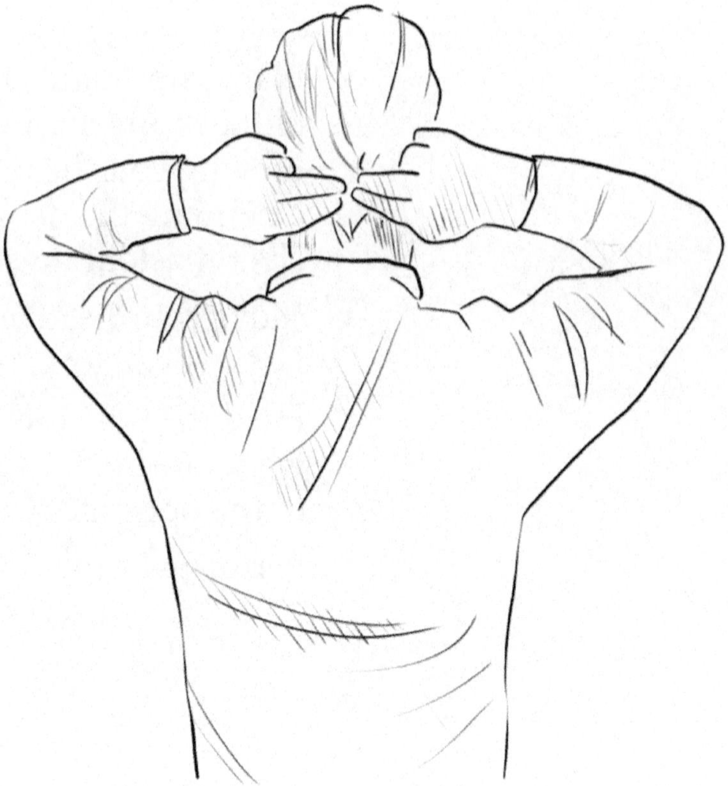

- Using middle and index finger, place the fingers of both hands in the dimple directly under the occiput in the sub-occipital muscles (under the nape of the neck)
- Push as hard as you can by making small circular movements with your head

Neck stretch

- Place your hands in a fist on your kidneys and arch your back while moving your head backward, thus extending the neck and the sterno-cledomastoid muscle
- Move your head and gaze side-ways as you lower further
- Hold the position 30 seconds while breathing deeply and repeat in the opposite side
- Perform 4 times on each side

This exercise is helpful in correcting posture moving the back, neck and abdominals

Neck stretch forward

- Sit on the floor on your heels resting your knees on the floor keeping your back straight and lower your chin to your chest
- Using a towel or exercise band, holding it from the ends with both hands, pass it over the back of the neck and apply gentle diagonal pressure until you feel the right amount of stretch
- Hold the position 15 seconds while breathing normally and repeat 10 times

This is a great exercise to relax and stretch the neck area, great for neck pain sufferers

Neck twist

- Sit on the floor crossing your legs, place both hands on your knees while keeping your arms relaxed, your back straight and your gaze forward
- Move your neck from side to side slowly coordinating your breath 5 times per side, then repeat 3 times

This exercise is also great for training the perception of space for anyone who suffers from balance problems

Gaze inversion

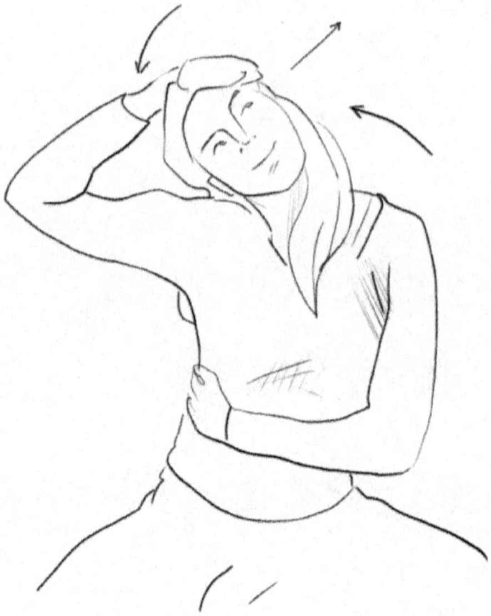

- While sitting, (you can sit on a chair or on the floor depending on how you feel most comfortable) bring the left hand to the right side of the torso, directly on the ribs and the right hand up to the left side of the neck
- Lower the head sideways by bringing the right ear to the right shoulder without straining while with the right hand you exert a slight pressure compressing the ribs inwards
- Breathe while holding the position for a few seconds, then move your gaze up to the left
- Hold this position for another 30 seconds, then repeat the exercise on the opposite side

BREATHING EXERCISES

Breathing exercises are a simple and effective way to stimulate the vagus nerve. In this chapter, we'll introduce a series of breathing exercises that can help to activate the parasympathetic nervous system and promote relaxation.

Neck lift

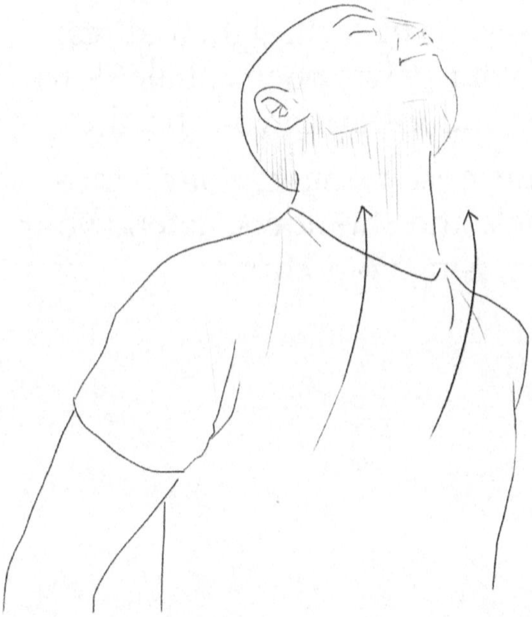

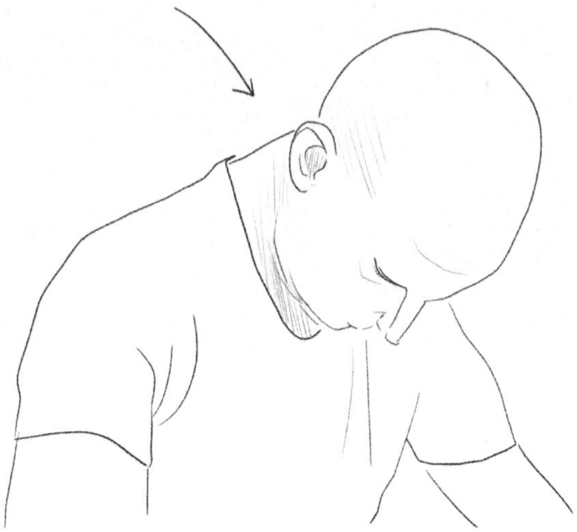

- Sit in a chair keeping a space of about 8 inches from the back, keeping your back and neck straight and feet flat on the floor
- Coordinating your breathing, raise your neck and head, expand your chest as you inhale and lower your head as you exhale, lowering your neck and shoulders accordingly.
- Try to keep a steady rhythm by taking 6 breaths and repeat for 3 sets

Great for stretching the back and front muscles of the neck

Breathing lotus

- Sit on the floor with your legs crossed, keep your back straight and rest your hands on your thighs at the height of your pelvis, then exhale slowly moving your hands forward on your thighs and lowering your head.
- Close your eyes and inhale deeply from your nose bringing your hands back to the starting position, open your chest and shoulders, extend your neck and move your head backward while raising your chin

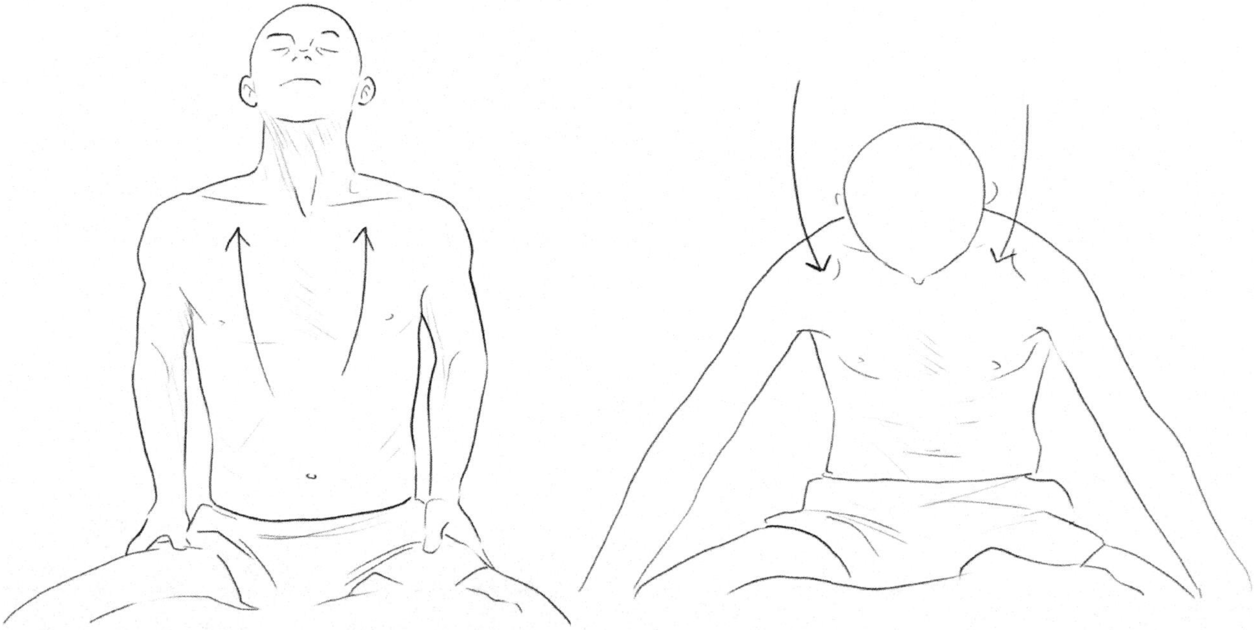

- Hold your breath a few seconds, now exhale deeply lowering your neck and shoulders moving your hands forward, then inhale again opening your chest and shoulders coming up again
- Inhale and exhale deeply repeating the movement for 30 seconds trying to find our own right rhythm but still trying anyway to perform it as fast as possible

- Once 30 seconds have elapsed, inhale as deeply as you can, and performing the same movement while moving forward, exhale retracting the navel
- Hold your breath until you feel the lack of oxygen, do not force it, throw out the air and inhale again returning to apnea for at least another 15 seconds

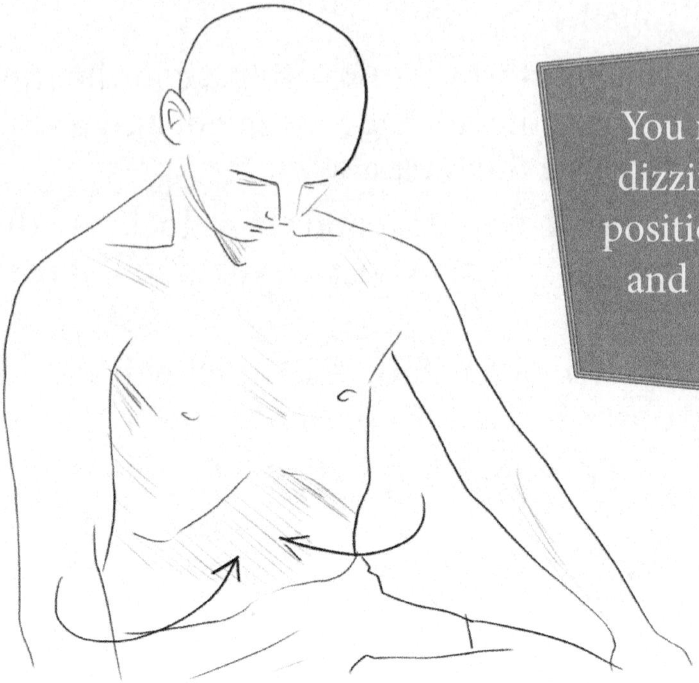

You may experience a feeling of dizziness, in which case you can position yourself in front of a wall and lean your back against it at this stage

- Throw the air out and return to relaxed breathing while keeping your back and neck straight for another 30 seconds
- Repeat the sequence 3 times

Arms swing

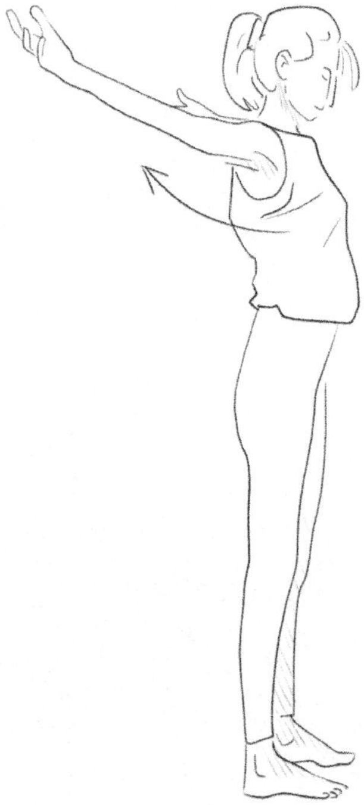

- Starting from a standing position Standing upright, keep your neck and torso straight and legs slightly open with parallel feet relined forward
- Linger in this position for 30 seconds, keep your eyes closed and take a few deep breaths
- Now perform arm rotations, coordinating the breath with the movement and trying to move them parallel.
- Perform for 30 seconds in a clockwise direction, then reverse the direction of rotation
- After also finishing the exercise in the opposite direction, continue by performing swing arcs with the arms for another 30 seconds
- Perform the sequence 3 times

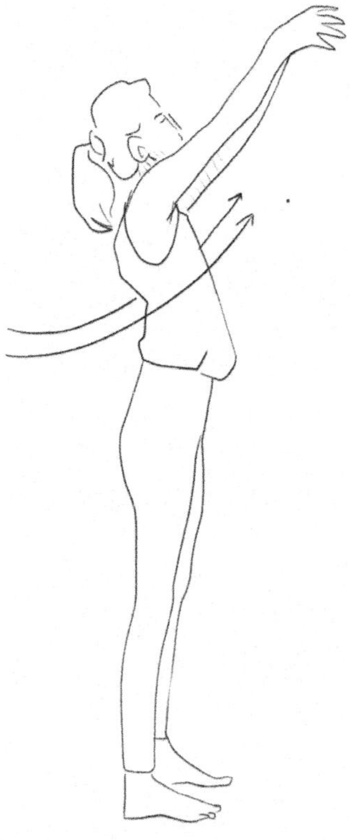

This exercise is useful for strengthening and mobilizing the muscles of the lower abdominals, and groin muscles(adductors)

BACK & HIPS EXERCISES

Hip exercises can indirectly benefit the vagus nerve by helping to relieve stress and tension in the body.

When the hips are tight and restricted, it can cause discomfort and stiffness throughout the body, which can activate the sympathetic nervous system, the body's "fight or flight" response, this can lead to an increase in stress hormones such as cortisol, which can negatively impact the body's overall health and well-being.

On the other hand, exercises that help to open up and release tension in the hips can activate the parasympathetic nervous system, which is closely linked to the vagus nerve and helps to promote relaxation and calm, this can help to reduce stress and improve overall physical and mental health.

Trunk twist

- ▷ Keep your feet resting on the ground at a 45-degree angle with your legs open, your butt placed inside your heels raised off the ground, and place your hands on the ground in front of you so as to support the weight of your body bringing us into malasana position (garland pose)

- For greater results you can perform this exercise without placing your hands on the floor

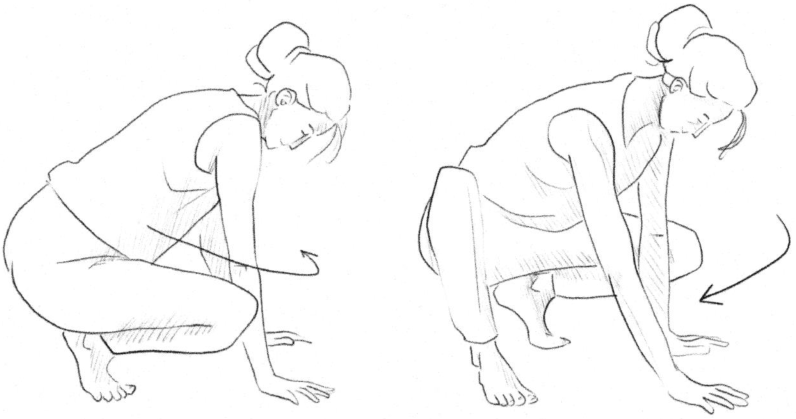

- ▷ From this position, start swinging from right to left coordinating your breath, moving your legs from side to side parallel, lowering your right knee moving it inward and raising your left by opening your left leg when moving to the left and vice versa when moving to the opposite side
- ▷ Perform 10 rotations for 3 sets

Hanging arms

- Standing, keep your legs slightly open, knees slightly bent and feet parallel
- As you inhale and exhale, slowly drop your body weight downward while relaxing your neck
- Cross your arms by grasping your elbows while keeping your head inside them
- From this position swing your arms from side to side accompanying the movement with your torso for 30 seconds
- Repeat the exercise 3 times

This exercise is useful for strengthening and mobilizing the muscles of the lower abdominals, front and back thigh (rectus and biceps femoris) and groin (adductors)
Great also for mobilization of the knee altriculation.

Torso twist

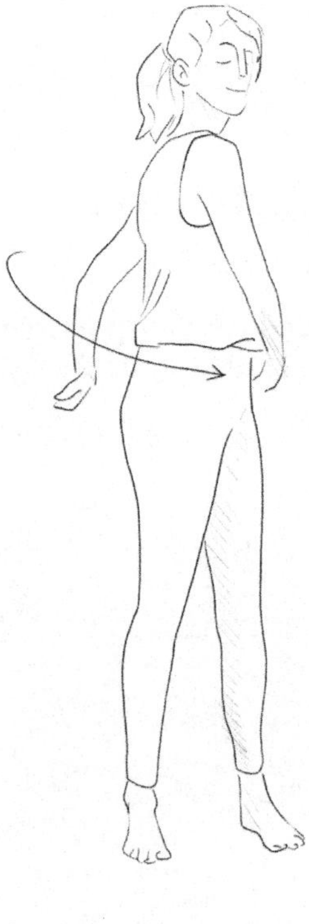

- Standing up, hold your legs slightly open with your parallel feet relined forward and let your arms fall down your body while keeping your eyes closed
- Reopen your eyes and breathing normally, perform torso rotations from side to side for 30 seconds accompanying the movement with relaxed arms
- Perform the exercise 3 times

Shoulders lift

- Starting from a standing position Standing upright, hold your legs slightly open with your parallel feet riled forward, inhale and exhale drop your arms downward slowly lowering your torso and head

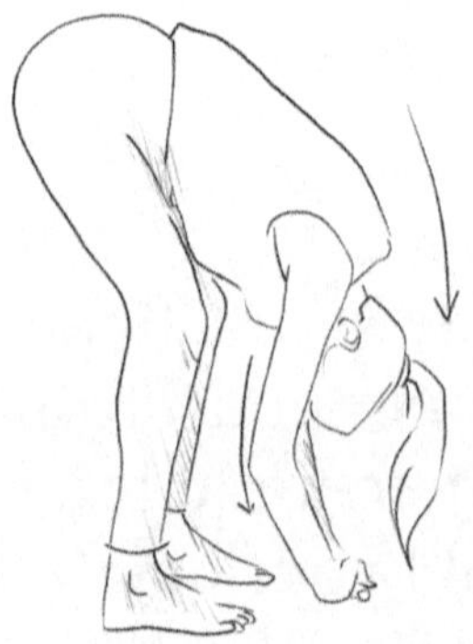

- Once you reach the point at maximum stop without straining, from here inhale and exhale performing 10 small forward strokes coordinating your breath

- Once finished return to the starting position slowly inhaling in a relaxed manner, keeping the neck and shoulders relaxed, after which repeat 3 times

This exercise is useful for strengthening and mobilizing the muscles of the lower abdominals, front and back thigh (rectus and biceps femoris) and groin (adductors)
Great also for mobilization of the knee altriculation.

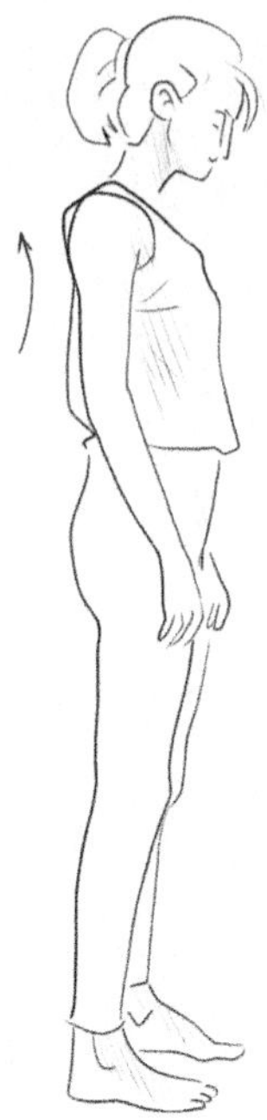

Abdomen tap

- Standing up, take a deep breath and hold it, tap your entire upper body, from the ribcage to the abdomen for at least 30 seconds, if you can't hold your breath longer than this, don't force it and catch your breath
- Once the 30 seconds are over, catch your breath and perform again
- Perform for a total of 4 repetitions

This exercise is useful for strengthening the front part of the thigh (rectus femoris muscle) and lower abdominals

Bridge

- Lie on your back keeping your arms along your body, legs bent and feet flat on the ground
- Raise your pelvis and place an exercise ball directly under your sacrum
- Now breathe deeply with your belly, keep your eyes closed and hold this position for 2 minutes

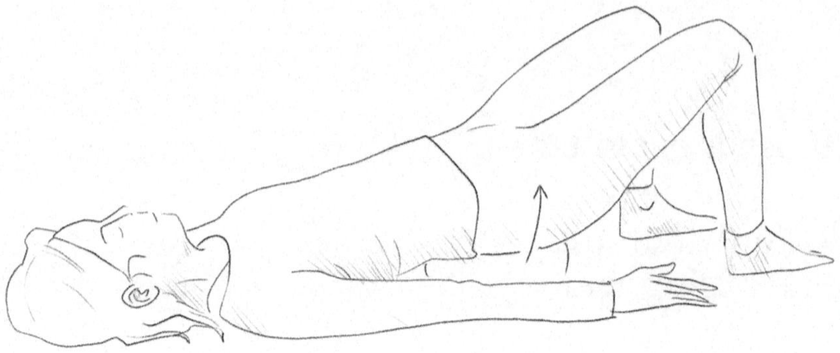

Useful also to mobilize and strengthen the muscles of the upper legs and lower abdomen; Mobilize arms and shoulders

Half push up

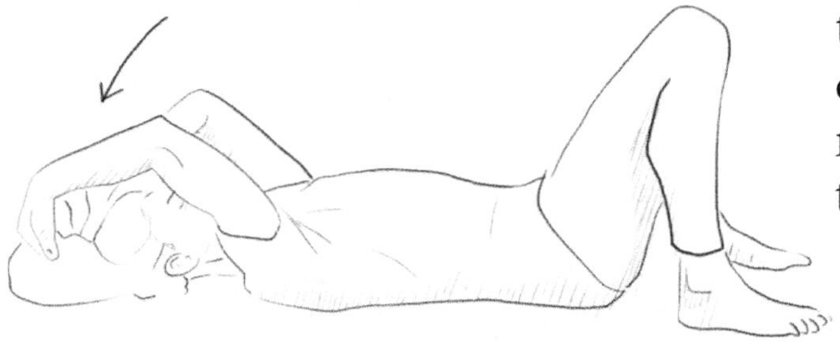

- Sit on the floor with your knees bent and both feet resting on the floor
- Slowly lower your back resting on the floor one vertebra at a time coming to place on the back of your neck while keeping your arms extended along your body

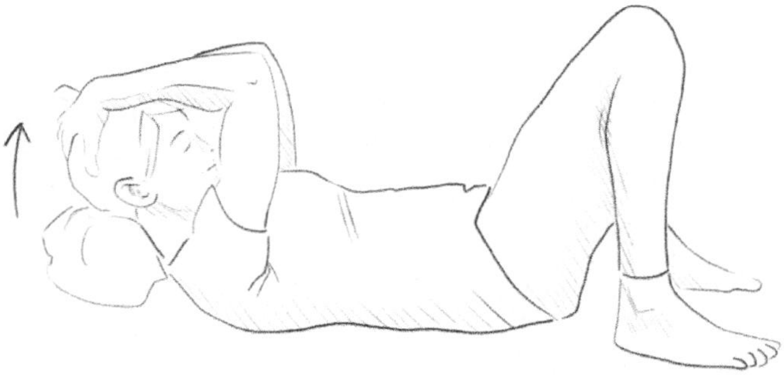

- Bring both hands behind the back of your head, inhale, and exhale slowly pushing your head up raising your shoulders

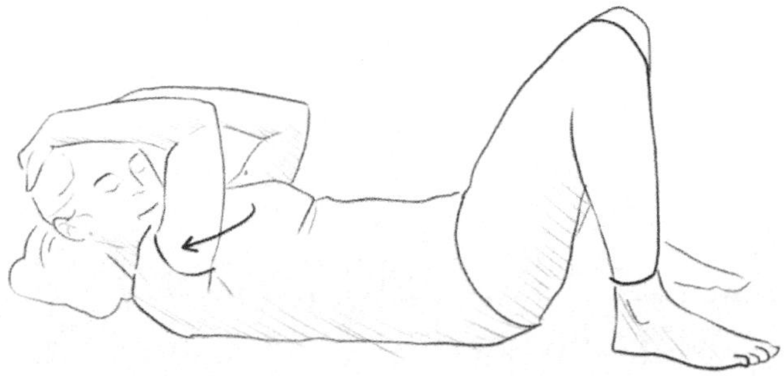

- Hold the position a few seconds, then rotate your head from side to side coming to rest your forehead on your forearm
- Performing 10 rotations
- Perform for 3 sets coordinating the breath

Great exercise to strengthen the upper\lower abdominals, correct posture and stretch the neck

VOCAL EXERCISES

Chanting and singing have been used for centuries as a way to promote relaxation and spiritual wellbeing. In this chapter, we'll look at the ways in which these practices can stimulate the vagus nerve and enhance our body's natural calming system.

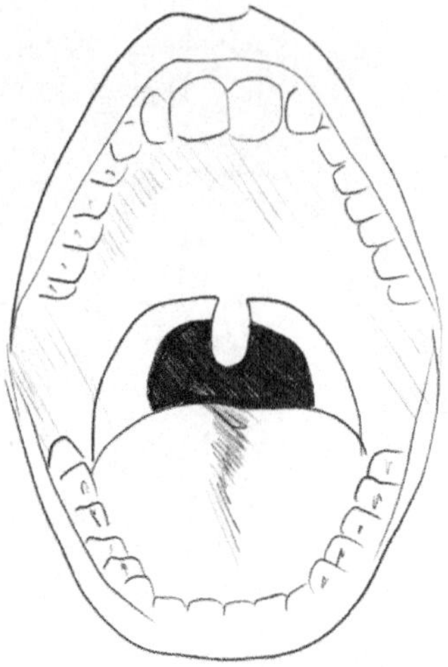

Vocalism

- While seated, perform distinct vocalisms after taking a deep breath
- The promo vocalism we will perform will be "Car", keeping the vowel for the whole time of exhalation
- The second one will be "Mom"

These vocalisms produce different internal vibrations that each stimulate different parts of the body, including organs and nerves. In addition, the vibrations stimulate the ramifications of the vagus present in the jaw and neck, reaching up to the stomach

Blind bee

- Place the two middle fingers, the middle and ring fingers on the eyes, the index finger on the forehead, the little finger on the cheeks and the thumb inside the ear using both hands

- Inhale deeply, hold for a few seconds, after which keeping the mouth closed makes vibrations producing a sound similar to the buzz of a bee until the air ends
- repeat for 5 times

Deaf bee

- Place both thumbs inside each ear using both hands, close your eyes and relax for a few seconds

- Inhale deeply, hold for a few seconds, after which keeping the mouth closed makes vibrations producing a sound similar to the buzz of a bee until the air ends
- repeat for 5 times

BELLY EXERCISES

Good belly exercises can help to activate the diaphragm, which is a muscle that is closely connected to the vagus nerve. The diaphragm plays an important role in breathing and helps to regulate the body's response to stress.

When you breathe deeply and diaphragmatically, you activate the parasympathetic nervous system, which is closely linked to the vagus nerve. This can help to promote relaxation and reduce stress levels in the body.

Abdomen breathing

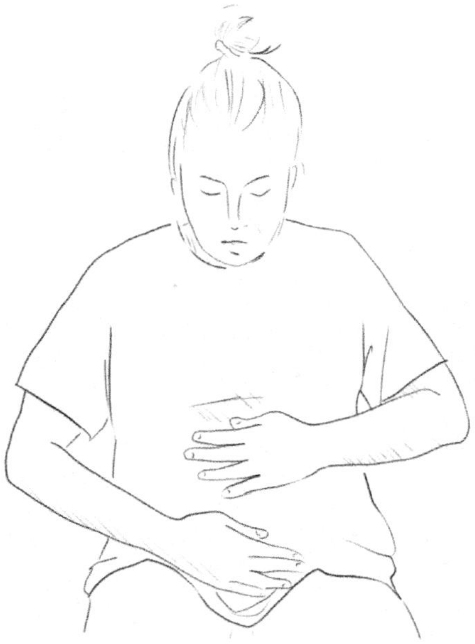

- While sitting, (you can sit on a chair or on the floor depending on how you feel most comfortable) keep your back straight and place your left hand directly on the upper part of the belly (at the height of the diaphragm) and the hand in the lower part
- Close your eyes and relax by breathing normally for a minute
- Now, taking slow, deep breaths, start tapping your belly with both hands as you breathe
- Perform 50 tappings, then repeat one more time

Abdomen massage

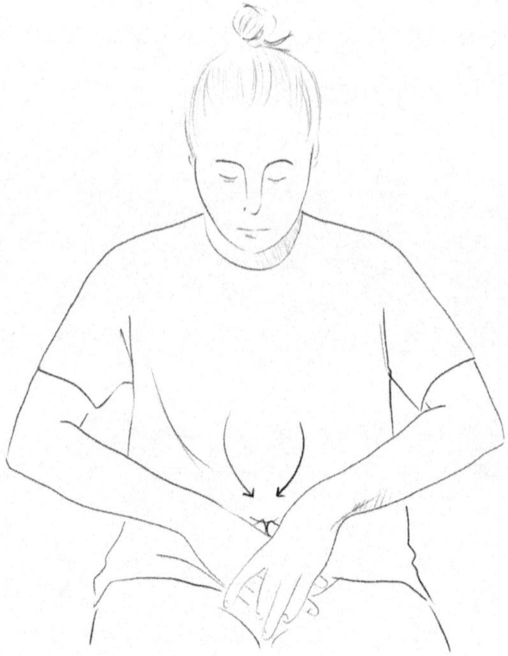

- ▹ Sit in a chair and keep your back straight
- ▹ Place both thumbs on the inside of your lower abdomen
- ▹ Breathe in and out at a brisk pace as you push the belly in with both thumbs 30 times
- ▹ Repeat for one more time

Chair walking

- Sit in a chair and keep your back straight
- Keep both arms bent at 90 “and close your hands into fists, then perform 30 side-to-side rotations following the movement with your arms keeping your torso straight, trying to coordinate your breathing
- Once finished, repeat one more time

Useful for mobilizing and strengthening upper leg muscles and lower abdominal muscles

Cobra position

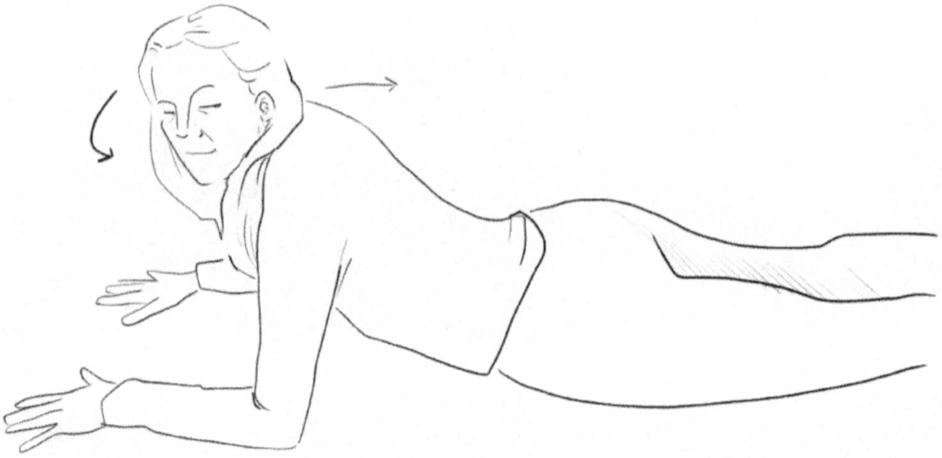

- Lie on your stomach, support yourself on your elbows keeping your hands open on the floor so that you can keep your upper body up
  Keep your elbows at shoulder height and breathing normally, rotate your neck to the left moving your gaze over your left shoulder
  Hold the pose for 30 seconds and repeat on the opposite side
  Repeat this exercise 3 times each side

This exercise is useful for strengthening the buttocks and lower back muscles

Butterfly

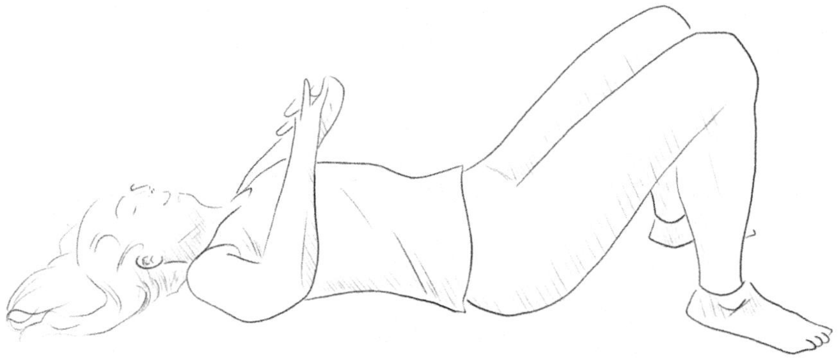

- Lie on your back, keep your legs bent and feet flat on the floor
- Interlace your fingers, bring them behind your neck and breathe deeply for a few seconds
- Now, keeping the head straight and the nose pointing up, move both eyes from right to left and from left to right holding the position a few seconds on each side
- Perform for one minute, then repeat one more time

Lying on the side

- Lie on your right side, rest your head on a rise or support using for example a yoga block and extend your right arm forward keeping it on the ground
- Using a gymnastic ball, place it in the lower part of the abdomen without pear, lean on the whole body but placing it in front of you, move part of the weight of the torso on it
- Place your left hand on your left hip at the height of the ball, then apply light pressure from top to bottom while breathing normally for 1 minute, then perform on the opposite side

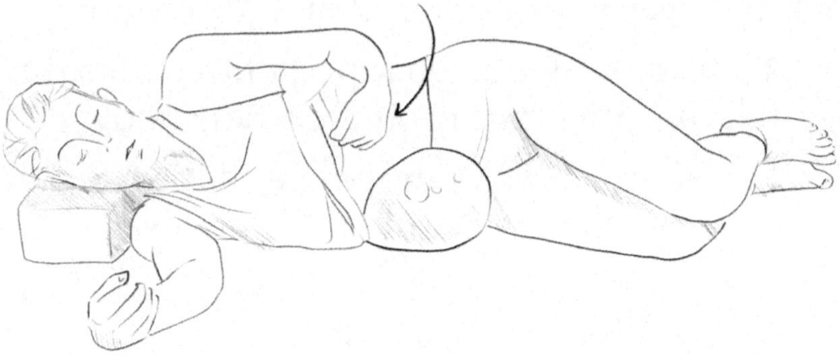

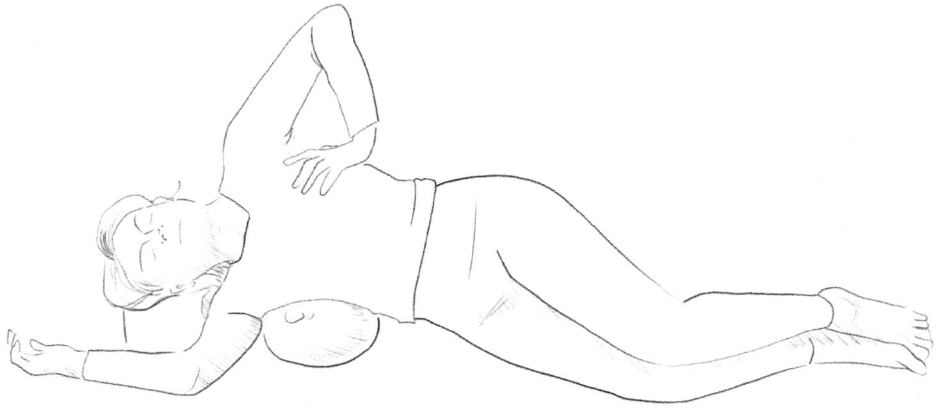

- Lie on your right side, rest your head on a rise or support using for example a yoga block and keep your right arm on the ground
- Using an exercise ball, place it in the upper part of the torso directly under the rib cage, but this time resting on the whole body
- Place your left hand on your left hip at the height of the ball, and breathe deeply for 1 minute, then perform on the opposite side

Lying down on the belly

- Lie on your stomach and place an exercise ball directly under your breastbone, cross your arms forward grabbing your elbows and rest your forehead on your forearms
- Breathe deeply trying to expand your rib cage as much as possible for one minute

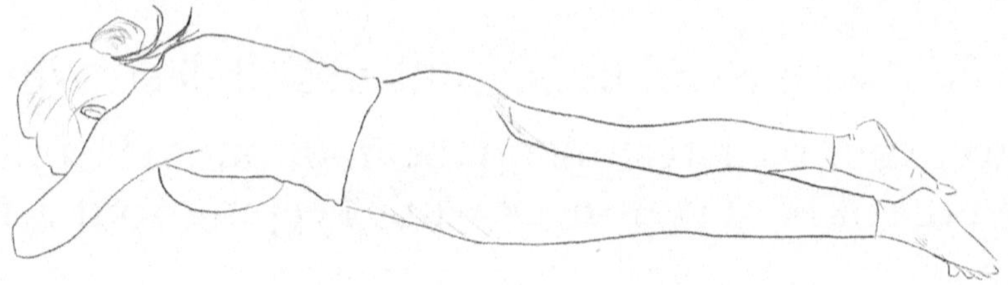

This exercise is useful for strengthening the front part of the thigh (rectus femoris muscle) and lower abdominals

Lying arms raise

- ▹ Sit on the floor with your knees bent and both feet resting on the floor
- ▹ Slowly lower your back resting on the floor one vertebra at a time coming to place on the back of your neck while keeping your arms extended along your body
- ▹ Inhale, bring both arms above your head, hold your breath for a few seconds, then exhale move your arms forward keeping them straight
- ▹ Hold this position for a few seconds, then bring your arms back over your head while inhaling and repeat the movement 5 times
- ▹ Repeat the sequence 3 times

This exercise is useful for
Strenghten and mobilizing lower abdominal
and the back

Exercises

for your health

INSOMNIA

There's some evidence to suggest a possible relationship between the vagus nerve and insomnia.
For example, one study showed that vagus nerve training can improve the quality of sleep in some people with sleep disorders. However, more research is needed to fully understand this relationship and to develop effective treatments for insomnia based on the basis of the vagus nerve.
Here are a few exercises that can help you:

- Half tortoise pose (28)
- Gaze inversion (35)
- Blind bee (51)
- Butterfly (58)
- Lying on the side (59)
- Lying down on the belly (61)

STTRESS RELIEFE

When the vagus nerve is activated, i.e. stimulating it, it can help reduce stress levels and counteract the effects of the sympathetic nervous system, which is responsible for the body's "fight or flight" response.
Chronic stress can negatively impact the vagus nerve, reducing its function and activity. This can lead to an imbalance in the autonomic nervous system, with overactivity of the sympathetic nervous system and underactivity of the parasympathetic nervous system.
Reduction in vagal tone, or vagus nerve activity, has been associated with a number of adverse health outcomes, including anxiety, depression and increased risk of cardiovascular disease. Additionally, studies have found that vagus nerve stimulation can help reduce stress levels and improve mood.

There are several ways to help stimulate the vagus nerve and improve its function, namely some of these exercises include deep breathing exercises, meditation, yoga and other relaxation techniques.

- Ear massage 1 (24)
- Ear massage 2 (25)
- Ear stretch (26)
- Shoulders lift (45)
- Abdomen tap (46)
- Breathing Lotus (38)

DEPRESSION

Research has found that individuals with depression may have reduced vagal tone or reduced vagus nerve activity. Reduced vagal tone has also been associated with increased inflammation, which has been linked to the development of depression. The vagus nerve helps regulate the body's immune response, and vagus nerve dysfunction can lead to increased inflammation and oxidative stress, and stimulation of the vagus nerve has been shown to have antidepressant effects.

Here are some exercises that may help:

- Neck twist (34)
- Breathing Lotus (38)
- Hanging arms (43)
- Shoulders lift (45)
- Half push up (48)
- Vocalism (50)
- Blind bee (51)
- Deaf bee (52)
- Lying arms raise (62)

DIGESTION

The vagus nerve, as discussed earlier, helps regulate the digestive system by controlling the production of stomach acid and digestive enzymes, as well as helping to move food through the digestive tract.

The digestive system and the vagus nerve are closely interconnected, with the vagus nerve playing a vital role in regulating digestion. When the vagus nerve is stimulated, it can trigger the release of digestive enzymes and increase the production of stomach acid, which helps break down food and aid in nutrient absorption.

Conversely, when the vagus nerve malfunctions, it can lead to a variety of digestive problems, including bloating, constipation, and diarrhea. In some cases, damage to the vagus nerve can even lead to conditions such as gastroparesis, in which food moves through the digestive system too slowly.

Here are some exercises that can help to stimulate it:

- Abdomen breathing (54)
- Abdomen massage (55)
- Chair walking (56)
- Lying on the side (59)
- Lying down on the belly (61)

NECK PAIN

When the vagus nerve is damaged or irritated, it can cause a range of symptoms, including pain and stiffness in the neck. In some cases, a condition called vagus nerve neuralgia can develop, which causes sharp, stabbing pain in the neck that can radiate to other areas of the body. In addition, some research suggests that the vagus nerve may play a role in the development of chronic neck pain. Studies have found that people with chronic neck pain have reduced vagal tone, meaning that the vagus nerve is not functioning as it should. This can cause a range of symptoms, including pain and stiffness in the neck and shoulders.

Here are some helpful exercises that can help to relieve the pain:

- Palm pressure (27)
- Neck turn (30)
- Cervice massage (31)
- Neck stretch (32)
- Neck stretch forward (33)
- Neck twist (34)
- Gaze inversion (35)
- Neck lift (37)
- Cobra position (57)

HEADACHE & MIGRANIES

Vagus nerve stimulation and other therapies that target the vagus nerve can also be effective in treating migraine. For example, some studies have found that breathing exercises that increase vagus tone can help reduce the frequency and severity of migraines.

It is important to note that although there is a connection between the vagus nerve and migraines, not all migraines are caused by problems with the vagus nerve. Migraines can have a number of causes, including genetics, environmental factors, and hormonal imbalances.

Here are some exercises that can help you relieve their symptoms:

- Ear massage 1 (24)
- Ear massage 2 (25)
- Ear stretch (26)
- Palm pressure (27)
- Neck turn (30)
- Cervice massage (31)
- Neck stretch (32)
- Neck stretch forward (33)
- Neck twist (34)
- Gaze inversion (35)
- Neck lift (37)

MENOPAUSE

During menopause, major hormonal changes occur that can affect the functioning of the vagus nerve. For example, fluctuations in estrogen levels can affect the vagus nerve and lead to changes in heart rate, digestion, and other bodily functions. Women who experience hot flashes and other menopausal symptoms, again, may have reduced vagal tone, which means the vagus nerve is not functioning as it should, and this can contribute to a range of symptoms, including fatigue, mood changes and sleep disturbances.

Some studies have found that vagus nerve stimulation can be a useful treatment for some of the symptoms of menopause.

For example, one study found that vagus nerve stimulation reduced the severity and frequency of hot flashes in menopausal women.

Below are some useful exercises:

- Arm swing (40)
- Shoulders lift (45)
- Abdomen tap (46)
- Bridge (47)
- Half push up (48)
- Chair walking (56)
- Abdomen breathing (54)
- Abdomen massage (55)
- Chair walking (56)
- Lying on the side (59)
- Lying down on the belly (61)
- Lying arms raise (62)

BRONCHITIS & ASTHMA

During an asthma attack, the airways become inflamed and constricted, making breathing difficult. The vagus nerve can play a role in this process, triggering the release of substances that cause the airways to become inflamed and constricted. Similarly, bronchitis is a condition that involves inflammation of the bronchi, which can impact breathing. The vagus nerve may contribute to the inflammation and constriction of the bronchi in bronchitis.

Although stimulation of the vagus nerve may be a potential treatment for asthma and bronchitis, it is important to note that this is an area of ongoing research and further studies are needed to fully understand the relationship between the vagus nerve and respiratory conditions.

If you are experiencing symptoms of asthma or bronchitis, it is important to talk to your doctor to determine the underlying cause and develop an appropriate treatment plan.

Here are some helpful exercises:

- Neck lift (37)
- Breathing Lotus (38)
- Arms swing (40)
- Vocalism (50)
- Blind bee (51)
- Deaf bee (52)
- Chair walking (56)

BACKACHE

While the vagus nerve does not directly connect to the lower back or spine, it can indirectly affect the muscles and tissues in that area. For example, if the vagus nerve is not functioning properly, it can cause digestive issues such as constipation or bloating, which may contribute to lower back pain. Additionally, chronic stress or anxiety, which can affect the vagus nerve, may also contribute to tension and pain in the lower back.

- Trunk twist (42)
- Hanging arms (43)
- Torso twist (44)
- Shoulders lift (45)
- Bridge (47)
- Cobra position (57)
- Butterfly (58)

Supplements

and diet advice

VAGUS NERVE HEALTH SUPPLEMENTS

Supplementation can be an effective way to support the health of the vagus nerve. There are a variety of supplements that may be beneficial for vagus nerve health, including:

- **Omega-3 fatty acids:** Omega-3 fatty acids, found in fatty fish and fish oil supplements, have been shown to improve nerve function and reduce inflammation, which can be beneficial for the vagus nerve.
- **Magnesium:** Magnesium is an essential mineral that plays a role in nerve function and muscle relaxation. Some studies have suggested that magnesium supplementation can improve vagal tone and reduce inflammation.
- **Vitamin B12:** Vitamin B12 is important for nerve health and function. Some studies have suggested that vitamin B12 supplementation can improve nerve function and reduce inflammation.
- **Probiotics:** Probiotics are beneficial bacteria that live in the gut and can help to improve digestion and reduce inflammation. Some research has suggested that probiotic supplementation may improve vagal tone and reduce inflammation.
- **Ashwagandha:** Ashwagandha is an herb that has been traditionally used in Ayurvedic medicine for its stress-reducing and nerve-supportive properties. Some studies have suggested that ashwagandha supplementation may improve nerve function and reduce inflammation.

VAGUS NERVE HEALTH DIET

It's important to note that supplementation should be used in conjunction with a healthy diet and lifestyle, and should be done under the guidance of a healthcare provider. Additionally, the effectiveness of supplements can vary based on individual factors you can support the health of your vagus nerve through diet. Remember to also incorporate a healthy lifestyle, including exercise and stress management, to support overall nerve health..

Here are some guidelines to follow:

- **Eat plenty of fruits and vegetables:** Aim to include a variety of colorful fruits and vegetables in your diet. They are rich in antioxidants and fiber, which can help reduce inflammation and support healthy digestion.

- **Choose healthy fats:** Omega-3 fatty acids found in fatty fish, nuts, and seeds can improve nerve function and reduce inflammation. Other healthy fats, like those found in olive oil and avocados, can also be beneficial.

- **Focus on whole foods:** Try to eat whole, nutrient-dense foods, such as lean proteins, whole grains, and legumes. These foods provide essential nutrients and can help reduce inflammation.

- **Limit processed foods:** Processed foods, such as sugary snacks and processed meats, can contribute to inflammation and negatively impact digestion. Try to limit these foods and focus on whole options instead.

- **Stay hydrated:** Dehydration can impact nerve function and digestion. Aim to drink plenty of water throughout the day to stay hydrated.

- **Consider probiotics:** Probiotics are beneficial bacteria that can help to support healthy digestion and reduce inflammation. You can find probiotics in fermented foods like yogurt, kefir, and kimchi, or you can take a probiotic supplement.

BREAKFAST

Starting your day with a healthy breakfast can set the tone for supporting the health of your vagus nerve throughout the day. Here are some breakfast food options to consider:

- **Whole grain toast with avocado**: Avocado is rich in healthy fats and fiber, which can support digestion and reduce inflammation. Pairing it with whole grain toast provides additional fiber and nutrients.
- **Oatmeal with berries and nuts**: Oatmeal is a great source of fiber and can help stabilize blood sugar levels. Adding berries and nuts provides antioxidants and healthy fats.
- **Greek yogurt with fruit and granola**: Greek yogurt is high in protein and can provide beneficial probiotics for gut health. Adding fresh fruit and granola provides additional nutrients and fiber.
- **Smoothie with spinach, banana, and almond butter**: A smoothie can be a great way to pack in nutrients and fiber. Spinach provides vitamins and minerals, while banana and almond butter provide healthy fats and protein.
- **Veggie omelet with whole grain toast**: An omelet made with veggies like spinach, peppers, and onions provides protein and nutrients. Pairing it with whole grain toast adds fiber and additional nutrients.

LUNCH

When it comes to supporting the health of your vagus nerve through diet, a balanced lunch can provide important nutrients and energy for the rest of your day. Here are some lunch options to consider:

- **Grilled chicken or fish with a side of roasted vegetables**: Grilled chicken or fish provides lean protein, while roasted vegetables offer fiber and antioxidants. Try roasting a variety of colorful vegetables like broccoli, bell peppers, and sweet potatoes.
- **Lentil or bean soup with a side salad**: Lentils and beans are high in fiber and protein, which can support digestion and reduce inflammation. Pairing them with a side salad provides additional nutrients and fiber.
- **Quinoa or brown rice bowl with veggies and chicken or tofu**: Quinoa and brown rice provide complex carbohydrates and nutrients, while chicken or tofu offers protein. Add a variety of colorful vegetables like carrots, bell peppers, and kale for additional nutrients and fiber.
- **Turkey or veggie burger with a side of sweet potato fries**: Turkey burgers or veggie burgers provide protein and nutrients, while sweet potato fries offer fiber and beneficial vitamins like vitamin A.
- **Whole grain pasta with tomato sauce and veggie**s: Whole grain pasta provides fiber and complex carbohydrates, while tomato sauce offers antioxidants. Adding vegetables like spinach, mushrooms, and zucchini provides additional nutrients and fiber.

DINNER

A healthy dinner can help support the health of your vagus nerve and promote overall wellness. Here are some dinner options to consider:

- **Grilled salmon with a side of roasted vegetables**: Salmon is rich in omega-3 fatty acids, which can reduce inflammation and support brain health. Pairing it with roasted vegetables provides fiber and antioxidants.
- **Stir-fry with veggies and lean protein**: A stir-fry made with a variety of colorful vegetables like bell peppers, carrots, and broccoli, paired with lean protein like chicken or tofu, provides nutrients and fiber.
- **Baked sweet potato with a side of steamed greens**: Sweet potatoes are high in fiber and beneficial vitamins like vitamin A. Pairing it with steamed greens like kale or spinach provides additional nutrients and fiber.
- **Grilled chicken or tofu with a side of quinoa and roasted vegetables**: Grilled chicken or tofu provides protein, while quinoa offers complex carbohydrates and nutrients. Roasted vegetables provide additional fiber and antioxidants.
- **Veggie chili with a side of whole grain bread:** A vegetable-based chili made with beans, peppers, and onions provides fiber and protein. Pairing it with whole grain bread provides additional nutrients and fiber.

IMPORTANT!

Remember to also stay hydrated and drink plenty of water throughout the day. By incorporating a variety of nutrient-dense foods into your dinner, you can support the health of your vagus nerve and promote overall health and wellness.

TIPS

for a healthy Vagus:

Incorporating healthy habits into your daily routine can help support the health of the vagus nerve and promote overall well-being.

It is important to remember that maintaining the health of the vagus nerve is a holistic process that involves taking care of your physical, emotional, and social well-being.

By prioritizing your health and incorporating these healthy habits into your daily routine, you can support the health of the vagus nerve and promote overall wellness.

Here are some healthy habits you can adopt to promote a healthy vagus nerve:

• **Practice deep breathing**: Deep breathing exercises, such as diaphragmatic breathing, can help stimulate the vagus nerve and promote relaxation. Slow, deep breaths can activate the parasympathetic nervous system, which can help reduce stress and anxiety.

• **Exercise regularly**: Regular exercise can help reduce inflammation, improve heart health, and promote overall well-being. Exercise can also stimulate the vagus nerve, which can help regulate various bodily functions.

• **Eat a healthy diet**: A diet rich in whole foods, such as fruits, vegetables, and lean proteins, can help support the health of the vagus nerve. Additionally, foods rich in omega-3 fatty acids, such as fatty fish and nuts, can help reduce inflammation and support nerve health.

- **Practice mindfulness**: Mindfulness practices, such as meditation and yoga, can help reduce stress and promote relaxation. Mindfulness can also stimulate the vagus nerve, which can help regulate bodily functions.

- **Get enough sleep**: Sleep is essential for overall health, including the health of the vagus nerve. Lack of sleep can lead to increased stress, inflammation, and decreased immune function. Aim for seven to eight hours of sleep each night to support the health of your vagus nerve.

- **Practice social connection:** Positive social interactions can help stimulate the vagus nerve, which can promote feelings of relaxation and well-being. Make an effort to connect with loved ones, join a social group or club, or engage in activities that bring you joy and allow for positive social interactions.

• **Reduce exposure to toxins**: Toxins such as pollution, pesticides, and chemicals can have a negative impact on the health of the vagus nerve. Take steps to reduce exposure to toxins by using natural cleaning products, avoiding processed foods, and limiting exposure to environmental pollutants.

TRACK YOUR PROGRESS

A good way to train yourself and get benefits is to keep track of your workouts.
This will make it easier for you to realize your progress or if something is wrong.
Below you will find some tables that will help you keep a "Diary" of your workouts in a simple way, you will have to report every time;

- **The day you trained**
- **Program type**
- **The time taken**
- **How do you feel** at the end of the workout
- And useful notes such as: "Today I skipped this exercise because of a nuisance"

Track your progress and start developing your Vagus tone!

	schedule\day	timing	duration	feeling	notes
Monday					
Tuesday					
Whednesday					
Thursday					
Friday					
Saturday					
Sunday					

	schedule\day	timing	duration	feeling	notes
Monday					
Tuesday					
Whednesday					
Thursday					
Friday					
Saturday					
Sunday					

	schedule\day	timing	duration	feeling	notes
Monday					
Tuesday					
Whednesday					
Thursday					
Friday					
Saturday					
Sunday					

	schedule\day	timing	duration	feeling	notes
Monday					
Tuesday					
Whednesday					
Thursday					
Friday					
Saturday					
Sunday					

	schedule\day	timing	duration	feeling	notes
Monday					
Tuesday					
Whednesday					
Thursday					
Friday					
Saturday					
Sunday					

	schedule\day	timing	duration	feeling	notes
Monday					
Tuesday					
Whednesday					
Thursday					
Friday					
Saturday					
Sunday					

	schedule\day	timing	duration	feeling	notes
Monday					
Tuesday					
Whednesday					
Thursday					
Friday					
Saturday					

Acknowledgments and Conclusions

As we have seen, the vagus nerve plays a crucial role in regulating many bodily functions and is intimately linked with our overall health and well-being. By understanding how the vagus nerve works and how to stimulate it through exercises and lifestyle changes, we can support our physical and mental health.

Throughout this book, we have explored the many benefits of vagus nerve stimulation, from reducing stress and anxiety to improving digestion and promoting better sleep.
We have also discussed the various exercises and techniques that can help stimulate the vagus nerve, including deep breathing, yoga, meditation, and more.

Remember, incorporating vagus nerve exercises into your daily routine takes practice and consistency.
Start with simple exercises, listen to your body, and gradually increase the intensity and duration of your practice.
Making these changes, you can support the health of your vagus nerve and improve your overall well-being.
I want to emphasize the importance of being patient and consistent when it comes to vagus nerve stimulation, the benefits of these exercises and techniques may not be immediate or obvious, and it can take time to notice improvements in your overall health and well-being.

However, with dedication and consistency, the benefits can be significant and long-lasting.

I also want to encourage readers to continue learning and exploring the many ways they can support their vagus nerve health.
There is still much research to be done on the vagus nerve and its connection to various aspects of health, and new techniques and exercises are continually being developed.
By staying curious and open-minded, readers can continue to optimize their vagus nerve health and improve their overall quality of life.
I hope that this book has provided valuable insights and practical tools for supporting the health of the vagus nerve.
By implementing these techniques into your daily routine and taking a holistic approach to health and wellness, you can support the health of your vagus nerve and promote optimal physical and mental health

And last but not least, a special thanks to my sister who inspired me to start understanding and exploring this topic first and a huge thanks to you for purchasing this book and helping to grow the community!
I hope this book can help you to get yourmind-body balance.

Bless You!

Suzanne Berggren

Vague and nebulous is the beginning of everything, but not its end.
(Khalil Gibran)

Here is your Bonus!

Scan the QR code below to get the download

DAILY

VAGUS NERVE

EXERCISES GUIDE

Printed in Great Britain
by Amazon

23669930R00064